Dean Firth

Bike Poems

Published in 2013 by jib-out

jib-out
18 Bridge Wharf
156 Caledonian Road
London
N1 9UU
jiboutdigital@gmail.com
www.jib-out.com

isbn 978-0-9926155-0-5

www.deanfirth.com

The right of Dean Firth to be identified as the author of this work has been
asserted by him in accordance with the Copyright, Designs and Patents act 1988.

Design and page setting by Fiddlenot
www.fidlenot.com

Printed in London by Print House Corporation
www.printhouse.co.uk

For my Dad, who has always used bikes as a way to show us his love.

old bike

Creature of rust, oil and dust,
time-battered lines of a fineness long gone,
reanimated to click syncopated
beats to the creaks of a rickety song.
Logical links and levers and spokes and
sprockets and brackets and brakes all but broken.

Brittle as bone or barnacled stone,
tension worked loose by the drowse of the dead.
Buckled geometry warped out of symmetry,
tortured to life from its tomb in the shed.
But a pining for pace, and the trace of a chase,
is a ghost in both pedals and handlebar brace.

Aching to turn, the two wheels yearn
to spin out their days a decay-fuelled dart.
Rheumatic skeleton craves the adrenalin,
last beats of blood through its oxidised heart.
But each judder and shudder of pothole and bump,
hasten the pace in the race to the dump.

cycling home
(with walt whitman)

The sirens and broken glass of Old Kent Road

The four-laned pressure of Elephant and Castle roundabout, demanding of the body that in order to survive it sprout new senses and become all-aware

The brief relief of an empty bus-lane or quiet back street

The breathless sensation of London Bridge—To the right:
Tower Bridge (a biscuit-tin parody olde England), Canary Wharf looming away in the distance. To the left: mismatched tangle of north Thames skyline, a train pulling parallel on Cannon Street Bridge. Ahead:
The City

Into the claustrophobic corridor of Cannon Street horizon rudely eclipsed by sheer verticals of concrete and glass

The impatient pulse of traffic

The orbic and stately geometry of Saint Paul's

The confusion of traffic lights, traffic cones, multitudes of merging roads and one-way systems

The seeming malevolence of trucks and blind bendy-buses like mythical monsters menacing a labyrinth

The pubs, the banks, the faceless chain stores and fast-food outlets of Fleet Street

Hordes of women and men in identical work costumes

The tall and narrow numberless passages leading off left and right into unknown London

The pomp and grandeur of the Royal Courts of Justice

The Strand, tree-lined Aldwych

Covent Garden with its clamour of theatres and restaurants and hapless tourists clogging the road

The seedy alleyway (a secret short-cut)

The shade of Shaftsbury Avenue

Centre Point, New Oxford Street

The flashing shrines to technology of Tottenham Court Road

Windmill Street

The casual opulence of Charlotte Street

Goodge Street

Cleveland Street

Home.

the ghost bikes

Sometimes a group of friends will take the mangled bike,
paint it white
and chain it to railings near the scene of the accident.
A kind of memorial.

—

I get these bouts of melancholy.
Though I'm gregarious by nature, I spend a lot of time alone.
Sometimes, at night, when the mood takes me,
I get so drunk I can barely see

and get on my bike.

I love it!
Abandon: self-propelled flight.
No helmet; black clothes; no lights.
Pulsing and flickering through the intense city traffic.

I prefer it when it rains.
Red traffic-lights and head lamps and street lamps blur.
The all-consuming focus of peril—
liberation from thought and self.

But these aren't suicide missions.
More a reckless expression of joy.

It's just that if that silver car
were to lurch its moment out of the darkness
and shunt into my side,
transferring force from fender to me
and then through my skull into the rainy tarmac,

the sensation of glistening asphalt
pressed cold to my cheek,
the landscape of dimming city lights,
the fading sound of sirens,
from this oblique angle

would somehow seem right.

chase

London that morning was humid and hot;
I'd had a big night and lucid, was not.
I was out of the plot
So when a friend said,
"Meet me in Bank for a beer,"
Cycling there probably wasn't the greatest idea.

Let me make it clear:
My cycling philosophy doesn't adhere
To government guide-lines, logic or fear.
The wrong side of the road is a fine place to be
And a red light to me
Is a mere suggestion,
Advice to be used at my own discretion.
And yes it's been said that I ride with aggression;
I'm a menace to myself and other road users.
Please forgive the digression.

Anyway, the clock on Saint Paul's said I was late
(A blatant result of my drink-addled state),
So I picked up the pace and that's when I saw,
Stopped at a red light, feet on the floor,
A bicycle cop.
I knew I should stop.
But I just thought, "Ah fuck it," and was off like a shot.
Right through those lights I flew;
The next set were red, and I shot through those too.
When from behind me I heard a cheap whirring sound
I thought it best to press on without looking around.
The dynamo siren got louder and clearer,
Meaning the cop was getting nearer and nearer.
Finally, he pulled along side
(I couldn't help but notice his massive backside).

I stopped.

He stopped.
And got off his bike sweating and panting,
Then came the ranting:
"Just cost you sixty pounds, that little stunt."
My best effort at sweet talk came out as a grunt.
"It's an on-the-spot fine. Have you got some ID?
Step off the bike son, come over here with me."
Now I'm no athlete, but I'm strong and I'm young;
This cop was about fifty and must've weighed half a ton....
The next thing I know I'm a man on the run!

My lungs and my legs screaming in pain,
The bottom of my jeans getting caught in the chain,
Through another red light like a runaway train,
And bloody hell! Here's that comical siren again!

And this time he's blowing a whistle as well!

This is it! I'm in a high-speed police chase,
A hung-over death-ride bicycle race,
With a sixty-quid-fine prize for second place.
So I'm up one-way systems, cutting up buses,
Up on the pavement, causing all manner of fusses,
Down little passageways twisting and turning:
Legs burning,
Adrenalin churning,
Breakfast on the brink of returning.

Soon as I think I've lost him,
And the chances of him accosting me
Seem lean,
I lock up my bike and flee from the scene.

Disorientated I wandered around
Till after ten minutes I finally found
My mate and got in a round.

It was time to head off after a couple of beers
And that's when the error of my ways became clear;
I knew that my bike must be somewhere real near
And a big chunk of iron can't just disappear:
But for two or three hours I wandered around
And the alley I locked my bike in was nowhere to be found.
All the while my headache getting worse and worse,
Right until dark I persevered in my search.
Finally, defeated, I went home on the bus
And then came back the next day for another good look.

So I do own a bike, it's a drop-handle Raleigh:
But it's chained to a lamp-post, somewhere in Bank, down an alley.

london labyrinth

Sing to me City, your Sibilant reel

    Mazes of Movement all Merge in the dash

    Classical Curves and the Concrete lines flash

Glint in the Glass and the Glimmering steel.

Treacherous Terrain, this Tumorous grid-

    Locked in the Limitless Line-up of wheels

    Orderless Ordeal of Automobiles

Crookedly Carving a Course through the mid

Cab drivers Carelessly Cut to the left

    Pedestrians Prance unexPectedly out

    Fossil fuel Fumes foul the Face, throat and mouth

Perilous Pathways exPand and compress.

    Smile as you Speed by, and Savour the view:

    Paralysed Porsches in Permanent queue.

crash

riding back from Ladbroke Grove
dark
raining
tired
bad mood

near Paddington
left turn round long bend
eyes right: London taxi
eyes left: steep curbed pavement
punter hailing

gap between pavement and cab
closing in slow motion
loads of time to think
"Down I go"

en route to ground
just enough time
to punch off taxi wing-mirror

cabbie shouts something about his mirror
shout something back about him being a blind old fucker
and lucky not to be dragged out of car and
shit kicked out of him

cabbie drives off
leaving punter stood on pavement
in the rain

salvage mission

I'm never quite sure about the ethics of doing this;
it's like I'm worried about accruing bad bike-karma.
Sunday afternoon: walking down a quiet backstreet to Regent's Park
carrying a green bag containing:
hammer, spanners, allen keys.

It's stupid really, this nagging concern.
I mean, these bikes have been left here to rot. No?
Long forgotten by their owners,
rusted beyond redemption,
wheels either nicked or kicked in.

Today I've come for a "new" crank.
The one on my battered old bike snapped
Thursday night on the ride back from Portobello.
And there it is, the shell I've reckied,
chained to a railing. Dismembered.

I wonder, at what point do these bikes become wrecks?
And what's the process?
I reckon it all starts with an opportunist wheel theft.
For how long does the owner still intend to sort it out?
And at what point does he give up on it entirely?

Is it when the remaining wheel's been stoved in
by a pissed-up lad?
Or once the chain's become a twiglet of rust?
Maybe he just lost the keys to the lock.

Right, the most important thing is—
you must studiously ignore the concerned
looks of passers-by. Motorists, dog walkers,
joggers and families out for Sunday strolls.
Do NOT imagine the scene from their perspective.

Try not to look guilty—the council
will just haul this junk into a skip
soon enough anyway. Surely?
And it's not as if it's a ghost bike.
If anyone asks, you say,
"This is my bike mate."
Oh my god! What if they say:
"No it's not, it's my bike."
Shit, come on, don't think,
just unfasten that bolt.

Right. Good. Ah, fuck.
I knew this would happen;
the bloody thing's rusted on.
Gets pretty hard not to notice those glances
when you're smashing the shit out of an old bike

with a hammer and all your might,
in broad daylight, by the side of
the busiest road in London...
And here it comes.
Yesss.

Put the crank in your bag
and confidently walk away,
head held high.
You have absolutely
no reason to look furtive.

the baleful ballad of the bike thief

Stories of stolen cycles resound
Lake-ripple like through this labyrinth town.
They merge and morph into myth-fabric yarns
And take on a terrible truth of their own.
But I have beheld him, the bike thief:
Countenanced his cowed and crooked form,
Witnessed your wheels whisked off to Brick Lane Market
And rescued my racer from his ranging grasp.
Some say that he has supernatural fluid
Beating through his black and beady heart;
I heard he was reared by rats in a rusty scrap-yard,
And some say he is scarcely man at all.
Here is the account of my encounter with this cunning wraith.

Solitary in the window seat I sat eating jerk chicken.
The gloaming dusk glinting on glass as I
Counted cars on Old Kent Road.
Locked to a lamp-post at my left I could see
My beautiful bicycle, bright in the half-light.
The jerk shop radio played reggae. A Rasta man
Came in to collect his curried-goat rice-and-peas.
The smoky scent of barbeque sweetened the air
And spice scorched my tongue as I savoured my meal.

The tinny tones of transistor radio
Were eclipsed by a clatter and clamour outside:
Approaching on the pavement and pulling a cart was a man,
Cap-peak pulled low, tracksuit collar pushed high,
Face hidden fully except for dark furtive eyes.
As he came closer I saw the contents of his cart
And the sight of it sickened my stomach with bile.
The trolley was piled with push bikes and packed with tools:
Big, brutal bolt-cutters,
Sharp and shiny shimmering saws,
And an angry-looking angle grinder.

The clunk of his cart came to a halt
And he stood still, staring at something:
Held an object helpless in his hard gaze.
A shiver of shock shook my spine
As he crouched and cradled my lock in his cracked palms.
My stomach lurched as I leaped from my seat and legged it out the door.

"Oi!" I said, as I stopped straight behind him.
Then, furiously, "What the fuck do you think you're fucking doing!?"
Not one little look up from the lock in his hand.
"That's my bike!" I bellowed to the back of his head;
The bastard seemed oblivious to all but the lock.
I shoved him to the shoulder and shunted him round
His malevolent eyes met mine for a moment and then
He sprang up and sprinted at speed down the road.

Bolting the barriers barring my path,
Darting dangerously through dense traffic,
I clung to his tail but could not close the gap.
Wiry and wild he was, like a
Sinuous sniper, spiked with guile.
The shape of his shadow shifting through the dark
Twisting and turning, trying to shake me.
Fired with ferocious anger, I followed his trail,
Breath burning my lungs, begging me to stop,
Streams of sweat stinging my eyes…
I was absolutely knackered, about to abandon the chase when:
He cut a crafty left, still caught in my sights,
And dipped down a dark alley.

Fatal flaw the fool had made
Stuck in a stale-piss-stinking alley
Barred between brick wall
And fucked-off, fist-clenching, fight-hungry Yorkshire man.

Cornered, he cowered by a bin and covered his head.
Rage-ragged breath ripped through my chest
And livid, I launched myself in a lunge at his jaw…
But my fist found only air where his face should have been,
And my carpals crunched into the concrete wall.

Confused in the clammy night air, I scanned around,
But found nothing, except on the floor of that fetid alley,
A black baseball cap.

Like a wisp of white exhaust fume on the wind, he was gone.

Back to my bike I bemusedly wandered,
Sweat-soaked shirt stuck to my back,
Mashed up mitt mangled and bleeding.

My bike was still safe outside the jerk shop,
But the tealeafing tool trolley was gone.

Nerves knocked, I navigated home one-handed,
Pondering the puzzling points of this riddle.

And from time to time I still catch a glimpse
Of a shadowy shape schlepping a cart.
And it saddens me when on a Sunday I see all the
Dubious deals being done on market stalls
Where bargain-hungry buyers beg no questions
And twisted traders tell no lies.
And thus are the perils perpetuated of owning a pretty bike in London.

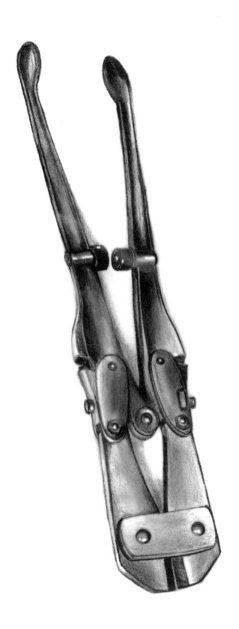

snow. bike. dustbin waggon

I'll start with the silence:
a city stunned and mute;
softness of snow
soaking up sound,
echoes captured
stifled to stillness,
motion muffled
powder-whispered patter.

And the darkness:
each street-lamp a prism of flurry in the dim
spotlight for the crystal drift,
crowded conical conduit
for unhurried but purposeful descent.

And me:
poor and ill,
winter-dishevelled.
Wretched.
Cycling to work through hauntingly blank
Bloomsbury back streets.

I slither forwards on the brink of traction.
No speeding.
No slowing.
No stopping or turning.

Held vertical by sheer force of stupidity.

The dustbin waggon at the crossroads
hulks its tons across the line,
its course and mine equally inevitable.

The silence intensifies
through the elongated breaking moment—
as the treacherous grip
splurges from under me in slow motion—
and then is punctured by the thud
and the crack
of the guitar on my back
crunching into
the (not-so-soft-after-all) road.

The cab of the wagon is lit with high-vis vests and faces
that look out on the dark and at me in the snow.

The equation for momentum is mass x velocity.

I swear that they're laughing as the truck glides on past.

a confession

Old Kent Road is the main route out of London to the southeast, which makes it an extremely busy road. It cuts through some of the poorest and most working-class areas of London. It's the cheapest street on the Monopoly board.

If you're there you're choked with car fumes, horns and engine noise, and you find yourself infected with the frustration that radiates from sluggish traffic.

A man on a bicycle – especially a crazy man with a flippant attitude towards the law and his own physical wellbeing – is by far the fastest moving thing on the Old Kent Road.

Down there the activity of lawless cycling can be re-imagined as an extreme sport, like white water rafting or base-jumping. You can have a lot of fun if you're stupid and young and reckless.

A confession: a shameful memory.

It is dusk
I'm going fast as fuck
sprinting the gaps between buses and trucks
spinning and ducking out then back in
headphones up full to blot out the din
my way through the mayhem a jaggedy line
I know the rhythm of each set of lights
I know the pulse and the pace of each junction
grit in my mind braced for one function
perception pushed to peripheral vision
stimulus triggers split-second decisions
focus unswerving I criss-cross the dark
jumping light's junction by Brimmington Park

Wheeling a folding shopping basket across the pelican crossing
safe under the watchful eye of the green man
in her late 40s or early 50s
a quite stocky West Indian woman

I slam on my brakes so hard when I see her
that I pirouette on one wheel
by the time that I hit her

But the impact didn't knock her down
She was quite a big lady
She stood there
with a look of hurt and disbelief on her face

I just carried on.

blind spot left turn

I remember the first time I told you I loved you:
all it took was a truck, your new bike,
and a spot of bad luck.

I remember your txt on my phone it said:
"Call me, I've been knocked off my bike."
So I called and you answered and burst into tears,

And the ambulance man took the phone and he told me
that you were ok, just a little shook up,
but the bike was a write-off,

So I ran up the road to UCLH A&E
to find you'd arrived just a bit before me
and I saw he was right, the ambulance man,

And your shiny new bike
couldn't possibly be any more bent or broken
and the only bit salvageable was the bell.

And when I went in you were there on the bed
and your clothes were all covered
in grease from the axle

And you cried when I held you
and showed me your grazes
and told me your story of under the truck,

How the ambulance men thought you must have been dead
when they saw your new bike
wrapped around the front wheel,

How you rolled out from under the truck
like a hero
and said you were fine to concerned passers-by,

How the truck driver came
and he brought you some water
and waited with you till the ambulance came,

Then the nurse cleaned you up
and we walked home together
and we lay on the couch and I cuddled you up;

But after an hour,
though it hurt me to leave you,
I had to get ready and hurry to work;

But you just seemed so sad lying there on the sofa
and I longed for some magic to make you feel better
and the words left my lips without my permission;

And the moment I said them
I knew they were true.

the frankenstein bicycle and the end of youth

And that was it. Who could predict it would manifest itself like this – on a dark night, on a quiet city street, in the form of a gigantic bicycle? A double-decker monster cruelly welded together in a steam-punk laboratory from dismembered body parts of rusted bike corpses. It was at least two frames high and the saddle was at least six feet off the ground. And not only was the crazy machine not locked up, but it also had a tatty piece of A4 taped to its lower cross bar which announced in felt tip writing:

'Free – please take.'

It was like a crazed inventor had plundered my unconscious! How could I resist?

But a strange thing occurred as I wheeled the bike to the nearest wall or bin or tree – anything tall enough to use as a mounting block. And the strange thing was this: I began to remember my drunken crash last year which had hurtled me into a parking meter and smashed my shoulder to pieces. I relived the strange smells and machines of the operating theatre and how badly my body had reacted to the anesthetic, and the numb patch on my left shoulder tingled at the thought of how warped my post-op posture had become.

More bizarrely still, I envisaged my unprotected skull swaying like a drunken pendulum ten foot from the tarmac and the contact crack of it echoing down this lonely street as I fell.

I thought of how cross my girlfriend would be.

And there and then, in that simple act of propping the Frankenstein Bike back against the wall, un-ridden, and continuing to walk home for my tea, youth ended.

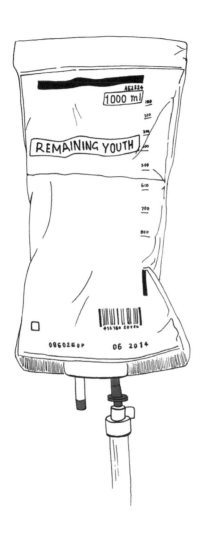

special thanks to

Sasha Langford: www.sasha-illustration.tumblr.com
&
Sarah Relf: www.facebook.com/TheMagpiesCabinet
For the wonderful illustrations.

Harry Akakpo and Lucinda Wherrett at Fiddlenot: www.fiddlenot.com
For the stylish and sensitive page setting and design – good work guys!

Naomi Booth & Duclie Few for their indispensable advice
and excellent work in editing the text.

Special thanks to the kind people at www.myriadeditions.com
who were the first people to publish The Frankenstein Bicycle
and the End of Youth in their excellent **Quick Fictions** iPhone/iPad
app, which you all should buy from the app store.

The online edition & links to the audiobook version of this collection
can be found at www.bikepoems.com

All poems by Dean Firth www.deanfirth.com